From the Small Business Primer Series

I0469438

Small Business Bootstrapping:

And Other Alternative Ways to Finance Your Small Business

by

Bob Foster

Copyright Page

Contact:
bob@business-solutions-and-resources.com

Website:
www.business-solutions-and-resources.com

Cover design by Dhyana Kearly
www.dhyzen.com

Small Business Bootstrapping: And Other Alternative Ways to Finance Your Small Business

Table of Contents

Books by Bob Foster

Be Your Own Turnaround Manager: A Common Sense Guide to Managing a Business Crisis

Business Survival Reality: The Mystery of Business Births and Deaths in the U.S.

Small Business Planning: How to Plan – Without Writing a Business Plan

Small Business Bootstrapping: And Other Alternative Ways to Finance Your Small Business

Small Business Financial Statements: What They Are, How to Understand Them, and How to Use Them

All books available at Amazon.com and other booksellers.

Introduction

This book is one of my *Small Business Primer Series*, and is directed primarily at the aspiring entrepreneur and the new small business owner — those who have little experience or knowledge about obtaining financing for their small business.

There are many, many ways to finance a business, either a startup or a growing business — and new ways are being added regularly. This book does not try to cover every single source of business financing, but rather the major concepts and avenues of business financing — with a few added tips.

Perhaps more important we will be looking at some alternative methods that are somewhat unusual ... the most notable being the concept of real "bootstrapping."

The term "bootstrapping" has been around for a very long time — so long in fact that the politically correct crowd prefers that we use the term *"organic growth."*

The problem here is that "organic growth" only works if there is something to grow from, while bootstrapping can work even when you are starting out with nothing except an idea and a passion.

So, we'll stick with the term "bootstrapping," instead of organic growth, in all our discussions in this book.

Most people who haven't tried it don't understand that obtaining financing is the most difficult part of starting and running a small business in the U.S. today.

Unfortunately, there are no hard and fast rules about financing our businesses — we are left to fend for ourselves … and that is what this book is all about.

To begin, we will delve into the challenges facing small business startups, as well as those businesses that are already operating but need more capital to grow.

Then we will go into the various avenues for obtaining small business financing — including alternative methods.

Lastly, we will look at the most difficult method for obtaining money to start a business — ***Bootstrapping!***

Chapter 1 —

The Challenge of Financing a Small Business

Considering the vast number of different types of businesses, it is obvious that not all small businesses have the same financing needs. The type of business you have will determine the avenue of financing available to you.

For instance, the sole proprietor of a consulting business will have different challenges than will a high-tech software corporation; and the clothes boutique owner will require different small business financing than will a machine shop — and so on.

In addition, the *stage* your business is in will also determine what form of small business financing you will need. That is, the startup will be looking at different financing sources than the business looking to finance growth.

Obviously, there will be some overlap between the various small business financing sources available to a wide variety of needs, and these will be discussed as we go along.

One Absolute Rule!

Before we go any further however, I want to caution every small business owner about the cardinal rule for seeking small business financing: ***You Must Be Prepared!*** It doesn't matter if you're hitting up your Aunt Matilda to help you start your kite store, or if you are presenting to a top tier Venture Capitalist — *you must be prepared.*

Here is what I mean by "being prepared":

*You need to be able to present an absolutely "knock-em-dead" description of your business and why it will succeed … **in 10 seconds or less**. Be prepared to recite this every time someone asks you what you do.*

This is to pique the interest of any of your listeners/readers so they will want more information. You might be surprised at where your startup money might come from.

After you get someone's initial interest — you need to be prepared with either a 30-second or 2-minute expanded story about your startup business, depending on the level of interest by your listener. You will need to do this when someone indicates they would like to hear more about your business.

If you are looking for financing from family and/or friends you should carry a copy of your "family and friends" Business Blueprint with you.

If you are looking for outside investment, you should always carry copies of your Executive Summary to hand out whenever appropriate (as long as it is well done).

NOTE: For more information on a "Business Blueprint" and an "Executive Summary," please refer to the *Primer Series* book, *Small Business Planning: How to Plan Without Writing a Business Plan.* (Available at Amazon.com and other booksellers)

The purpose of the items above is to convince your listener/reader that you know what you're talking about and that you have done your homework. No one is going to seriously consider listening to you if you stumble around trying to explain your new business. You want them to be attentive when you present your "pitch" for financing your business ... so make it the best you possibly can.

If you can do these things, and do them well, you should be able to finance your small business no matter what the economy is doing; what kind of business you have; or what stage of development your business is in.

Financing a new business is often the most difficult part of being an entrepreneur. It usually takes a tremendous amount of time and effort, and there is no simple solution ... unless you are independently wealthy.

Let's see if we can pin down what you will be dealing with when you start looking for your new business financing:

Smaller Small Businesses

This is primarily the small owner-operated business without employees. This category of business makes up the largest segment of U.S. businesses — approximately 22 million, or 70% of the total.

This is a category of American industry that deserves more attention, because these are the small businesses, all over the U.S., that may be working on the next great American Innovation. Actually, I'm sure this is true in every country around the world.

However, these businesses are too small to normally interest investors, and in their early stages are rarely "bankable" — so the primary source of financing is by you, the owner ... through "creative business financing."

Non-High-Tech Businesses

This can be any one of a variety of businesses, but the major categories are manufacturing, healthcare services, construction, food service, and retailer.

Historically, Venture Capitalists and Angel Investors have shied away from investing in non-tech businesses, but fortunately, that has changed somewhat with the more recent poor performance of high-tech startups. VCs and Angels are now listening to more non-tech proposals — and occasionally investing money.

All the resources for financing a new business, as discussed in this book, should be solicited for this category of startup.

High-tech Businesses

This category of business is the "darling" of American business, even though it is a small percentage of the total number of annual startups. Many authors, investors, academics and pundits seem to assume that when you say "startup," you automatically mean a "high-tech" startup.

Unbelievably, there are many twenty and thirty-something's that believe there was no such thing as a "startup" prior to the popular use of the Internet and high-tech businesses.

Writers glorify these startups, and investors want to invest money in them — all anticipating the next Google, Facebook, Twitter, or what have you.

This category of startup is the domain of Venture Capitalists and Angel Investors. These two groups of investors were created by the need of high-tech businesses for startup financing.

Interestingly, there have been many more failures than home runs for High-Tech investors, and that has caused many investors to start looking elsewhere for investment opportunities.

So, each category of business and each business within each category have a different need for financing.

Warning!

There is a set of unwritten rules that affects very new businesses — especially those searching for financing. These rules are:

> *— Your expenses will always be greater than you planned for.*

> *— Your revenues will be smaller and slower in coming than you planned for.*

> *— More things will go wrong than you ever imagined.*

> *— You can finance a new business with less money than you think you need. (Bootstrappers, take note.)*

> *— If you want to be an entrepreneur bad enough — you will find the money for financing your new business.*

It would be good if you committed these five things to memory and recalled them periodically as you go through your process of financing your business.

So, where does the money come from? The following chapters each detail the normal sources of small business capital, plus several alternative sources that many new business owners may not be aware of.

Chapter 2 —

Bank Business Loans

I'm sure you realize that banks do NOT ever "invest" in a business startup. Banks are in business to "loan" depositor's money, and make a profit in the process.

Moreover, banks do NOT "loan" money to non-established businesses (startups). They sometimes loan money to a new business founder (personally), if the founder has assets besides their business to use as collateral. Today, however, even this situation is a difficult sell to a banker.

Banks normally make business loans to help grow and expand successful businesses. Unfortunately, in today's economic climate banks might be the last place to look for money to finance most business endeavors.

With all the new government requirements for banks to raise their capitalization (keep their money themselves), banks are simply not making many loans to small business. Even some long-term bank relationships are being discontinued.

However, there are a few exceptions, because bankers are a fickle group, especially when it comes to small business bank loans. If you have a high personal credit score, a successful existing business, and substantial collateral, you might score a small loan.

Just make sure your pitch is better than it has ever been, and that it fits the requirements of the banker you are talking to. (Ask about their loan criteria before you present your business requirements).

If you need investor money, or venture capital, obviously, you will not get that from your bank—although a good banker should be able to introduce you to an Angel Investor or Venture Capitalist.

Also, much depends on the amount of money you are looking for. You and your banker may be able to find ways to make a bank loan of a few thousand dollars, but when you start looking for more—especially to start up a business—your chances for small business bank loans quickly diminishes.

How to Proceed with Your Search

Having said that however, if you believe you may qualify for any of the SBA loan programs, you will also need to apply through your local bank, or some other financial institution, in order to acquire an SBA guarantee.

If you have a good relationship with your local banker, this is always a good place to start, because even if the bank cannot make the loan themselves they usually can give you some good advice and may even steer you to other places that might be interested in financing your project.

So, here is the approach I am recommending today, regarding small business bank loans:

Start with the bank where you have been doing business the longest. If you have developed a business relationship with a particular banker, so much the better.

Make sure your personal credit is in good shape and your credit score is high.

Make sure you have lots of good physical collateral that you personally own.

Be absolutely clear on your need and purpose for the money you are asking for. Your Small Business Plan needs to be in tip-top shape, and your pitch razor sharp.

Look and act like you are a good loan candidate.

If the bank turns you down, be sure to ask for your banker's help in finding alternative contacts for your project.

Don't think there is anything wrong with either you or your business project just because the bank turned you down.

Make your pitch to all the banks in your area, because each bank tends to specialize in certain areas of lending, and where one bank may not have an interest in your project, one of the next ones you talk to might.

Keep trying, and approach each bank as though they were the first. And don't forget to ask each banker for advice on where else you might go to secure financing for your project.

In summary, it is difficult to obtain small business bank loans today, but you should still start with a good reputable lender in a bank large enough to support your business as it grows. You need to do this for the following reasons:

You need to have a strong banking relationship as your business grows.

Your banker can assist you in obtaining an SBA guaranteed loan, if this is something that fits your business project.

Bankers can often introduce you to Angel Investors and Venture Capitalists, if this form of investment better suits your needs.

If you are going to do an "owner financing business" method, your banker can still often help you.

My suggestion is to always start with your local banker, or banks in your area, regarding small business bank loans. Even if they can't make a loan to you directly, they may be able to use an SBA guarantee to make the loan.

Even more important, your banker should be able to introduce you to any number of alternative investors, including Venture Capitalists. If they can't (or won't) you are dealing with the wrong banker and should start looking for another.

In the next chapter we want to look at how banks work with the Small Business Administration (SBA) to help owners finance their small business.

Chapter 3—

SBA Business Loans

First, you need to be aware that the *Small Business Administration* (SBA) does NOT loan money directly to business owners. The SBA simply "guarantees" loans made by financial institutions to business owners.

Furthermore, the SBA will not guarantee a loan to an entrepreneur just because they want to start a business. Any deal the SBA is involved in must basically meet the standards set down by the lending institution requesting the guarantee.

However, since the SBA does guarantee loans to small businesses for expansion, or to buy an existing business, let's take a look at some of the details of what the SBA has to offer.

An SBA business loan is strictly for small businesses, so it is important to know what the SBA considers a "small business." The standard guide of 500 employees or less constituting a small business only applies to a percentage of identifiable businesses.

The SBA sets a guideline for *each* of the *North American Industry Classification System* (NAICS) codes. They have compiled these guidelines into a 44-page document … and here are just a few examples of what the SBA considers a small business:

A convenience store is considered a small business if it has $27.0 million, or less, in annual revenue.

A software publisher ... if it has $25.0 million, or less, in annual revenue.

A producer of chickens for egg production ... if it has $12.5 million, or less, in annual revenue.

A producer of chickens for meat consumption ... if it has $0.75 million, or less, in annual revenue.

A telecommunications reseller, is considered a small business if they have 1,500 employees, or less.

A cigarette manufacturer ... if it has 1,000 employees.

A Mineral Wool manufacturer ... 750 employees.

A Concrete Block manufacturer ... 500 employees.

The Wholesale Trade (all products) ... 100 employees.

So, you can see from these examples that there is a broad range of SBA definitions for what they consider a small business. As a result, your first task, when seeking an SBA business loan, would be to determine whether or not your business is considered a "small" business by the SBA.

To assist you in this, you can download the detailed document at this address: http://www.sba.gov/content/small-business-size-standards

Now, assuming you have determined that you do indeed have a "small" business, what kind of SBA business loan is available to you? Obviously, much depends on what stage of development your business is in—and for what purpose you need a loan.

Loan Programs

7(a) Loan Program

This is the most popular SBA business loan program, because it is very flexible and the money can be used for most business purposes. This program might be helpful to some startups—depending on how early the startup—but is particularly designed for existing businesses.

If you think your business may qualify for an SBA guaranteed loan, here is how I would suggest you go about applying for this SBA business loan.

Meet with your local banker and present your Business Plan in your most concise and convincing manner. Then discuss with your banker the various financing methods that may work for your project.

Depending on the status of your project or business, and the purpose of your loan, your banker should make some recommendations. (If your banker doesn't make recommendations and assist you — you have the wrong banker and you need to find someone else).

Here is what your banker should discuss with you:

Whether or not the bank can make the loan directly without an SBA guarantee.

If not, they should discuss the various SBA business loan programs available through their bank (most SBA business loan programs are available through most banks — but not all).

Your banker should arrange for the SBA application and assist you with the paperwork (remember, the bank is going to loan the money at this point and the SBA will only be the guarantor).

Your banker may, or may not, put you in direct contact with a SBA representative, but they should be overseeing the processing of the paperwork.

Have you sign the papers and then they will disburse the funds.

Or, if your banker does not participate in SBA business loans (some prefer not to), your banker should direct you to a bank or other commercial lender who does specialize in SBA loans, and you would then go through the process described above.

NOTE: If you cannot find a banker who will work with you, contact the local SBA District Office, and they can direct you to a commercial lender who handles SBA business loans.

There are also several restrictions on a 7(a) SBA business loan. This form of loan cannot be used for the following purposes:

To refinance debt where the viability of the business is in question, and the SBA may have to pay on the guarantee to the bank.

To finance a partial change in business ownership, such as buying out a partner.

To provide funds for the reimbursement to an owner, whether temporary (bridge loan) or long-term.

To repay delinquent state or federal withholding taxes, or any money that would be held in trust or escrow.

For any purpose the SBA deems non-sound.

Express Programs

There are several sub-categories of the 7(a) loan program you should know about. These are called "Express Programs."

SBA Express —

This program provides an accelerated turnaround time for review of your application by the SBA, who will give you a response to your application within 36 hours. This is not the complete processing of your application, just a review to determine if you have a chance with them or not.

It is best for smaller loans, so if you are near the top of their lending limit, I would suggest working through normal channels.

Export Express —

This SBA business loan was set up to help small businesses develop or expand their export markets. Most banks in the U.S. do not normally lend money on export orders, offshore receivables, or Letters of Credit (for export). This is where the SBA steps in and can provide lenders with an up to 90 percent guaranty on export loans.

The purpose of this sub-category of loan guarantee is to encourage banks to make loans that will help small businesses with their export market.

Lenders still use their own credit decision-making process and loan paperwork, and the SBA provides an expedited eligibility review and subsequent response in less than 24 hours. This allows small businesses to get access to their funds for exports faster.

Eligibility is the same as for all 7(a) SBA loans, but applicants must have been in business for at least 12 months to qualify for an Export Express loan guarantee, though not necessarily involved in exporting during that time. In addition to standby Letters of Credit, the money can be used for the same purposes as all 7(a) loans.

In this loan program, the SBA also provides export training and assistance to small businesses, including marketing, planning, and management assistance.

Again, application for this SBA business loan is made directly to the lender, although the lender must be a participant in the SBA Express Program. For more detailed information contact your local **U.S. Export Assistance Center** through your SBA District Office.

Patriot Express —
If your business is 51 percent or more owned by veterans or members of the military, you may apply to this program for expedited service. It is not a special lending program for veterans, only special handling of the loan application.

Community Express –

This program allows SBA approved bankers to provide a combination of financial and technical assistance to borrowers located in certain "underserved" communities, known as "Historically Underutilized Business Zones" (HUBZones).

This also includes communities identified as distressed through the "Community Reinvestment Act" (CRA). If you think your business may fall into one of these categories, contact your local SBA District Office for more information before going to your banker.

CDC/504 Loan Program

This is a specialized SBA business loan that can be used only for the purchase of assets or to pay for physical improvements. This too, is a government guarantee program, not a direct loan from the SBA.

The money cannot be used for working capital, investing, repaying debt, or refinancing.

If you are planning to acquire any major assets, or build some physical expansions, this loan guarantee may be just the ticket for you. You approach this SBA business loan exactly the same way as detailed for the 7(a) loan program. Only the purpose of the loan is different.

Micro-loans

This program provides short-term loans to small businesses and not-for-profit child-care centers. The maximum loan is $35,000, and the average loan is approximately $13,000. The SBA designates only certain intermediary lenders for this program and you must work through one of these designated lenders when applying for this special loan.

The money can be used for any business purpose except paying existing debt, or buying real estate.

These specialized lenders are also required to provide business training and technical assistance to the borrowers, who may also be required to complete training and/or planning requirements before the loan is considered.

Unfortunately, this program has not been very popular due to the excessive amount of paperwork and government bureaucracy involved. This is really too bad, because a program like this could greatly benefit many smaller businesses.

Other Programs

There are a few other programs available through the SBA, including one for disaster relief, and a current temporary program for financial relief. The SBA also offers special business counseling to assist veterans.

As you can see, the purpose of the loan must be convincing in the eyes of both the banker and the SBA; and you, the owner, must be creditworthy. As you can probably guess, the process for obtaining an SBA business loan is a long drawn-out affair that requires a great deal of patience.

At the same time, there are many instances where an SBA business loan is an excellent alternative to mainstream funding for your business. In some cases, it may be the best alternative you have.

You also need to know that the final decision is up to the lender, and if they say "no" anytime during the loan process — there is nothing the SBA can do about that. You will have to start over with another lender.

A Couple of Reminders:

First — In most cases, you need to start your search for a SBA business loan with your local bank. Then they will do one of several things:

Make the loan directly to you without an SBA guarantee, or…

Work with you to apply for the appropriate SBA guaranteed loan for your business, or…

Recommend another bank or commercial lender that specializes in SBA guaranteed loans, or...

Suggest other forms of funding that may be better suited to your needs.

Second — Be prepared. Every time you meet with a bank or talk to a representative of the SBA, you need to be on top of your game and have as many answers ready for their questions as you possibly can.

This chapter provides a brief summary of most of the SBA business loan programs available to small business, but they do change from time to time. If you want more detailed information on SBA guaranteed loans, you should contact your local SBA District Office. You can find their location in your local phone book, or online.

One of the more popular sources of small business financing today is the Angel Investor. We'll take a look at Angel Investors in the next chapter.

Chapter 4 —

Angel Investors

Angel Investors are generally affluent people who operate as independent investors in small businesses. Although they usually favor small startup businesses, some Angel Investors may also invest in currently operating small companies that are looking to expand.

Unlike Venture Capitalists (VCs), who invest other people's money from an investment pool, or "fund," Angel Investors invest their own personal money, although the legal investing entity could be a trust, foundation, corporation, business, or the like.

Angel Investors tend to fill the gap between self-financing (self, family & friends) and Venture Capitalists, who typically are not interested in investing the smaller amounts invested by Angels.

The total annual U.S. investment by Angel Investors is almost as much as the total amount invested by Venture Capitalists, but Angel Investors invest this much in many times as many businesses (which is still not a comparatively large number).

A New Partner

You must be aware, that these are not lenders — they *invest* in your business (although they may do both), and you will have a "partner" whether you like it or not.

Obviously, Angels invest in high-risk ventures, and face dilution of their equity if additional rounds of funding are provided by Venture Capitalists.

Consequently, these investors require a very high rate of return. This is why they demand a high-return exit strategy in your Business Plan — perhaps as high as 10 to 30 times their investment over a five to eight year holding period.

In recent years, individual Angel Investors have often formed *Angel Groups*, and networks of individuals or small groups. These groups are called "Super Angels" and are blurring the lines between Angels and VCs. Occasionally Super Angels can take a business all the way to an *Initial Public Offering* (IPO).

If you ever watched the TV program "*Shark Tank*," you saw Angel Investors (NOT Venture Capitalists) in action — Hollywood style.

How many Angel Investors are there? No one knows for sure, but the *Small Business Administration* estimates there are over 250,000 of these Investors operating in the U.S., funding about 30,000 small businesses. It is estimated that there are about 4,000 to 6,000 in the U.K.

However, because of the privacy of individual investors, very little is really known statistically.

Who Are Angel Investors?

Often they are retired business people, or affluent executives. In many cases these investors are as interested in the "process" of Angel Investing as they are in the money. They feel they have something to offer as mentors and coaches, and in many cases they fill an important non-financial need in the small business they invest in.

However, there are requirements for becoming a professional investor. All Angels must be "accredited" investors, as required by Regulation D of the *Securities and Exchange Commission* (SEC).

This is to assure that the investor is financially sophisticated and is unlikely to create long-term issues for the economy.

To be accredited, an investor must have a net worth exceeding $1 million, either individually, or jointly with their spouse (excluding the value of their residence). Or, earn an income of $200,000 per year individually — $300,000 joint income — in each of the past two years, with the expectation that level of income will continue in the current year.

Requirements for trusts are somewhat higher.

Who Do Angels Invest In?

They typically invest in high potential startup businesses, usually with fewer than 20 employees. They also like to invest close to home so they can keep an eye on their investment.

That means the farther from home you look for an Angel investor, the more you reduce your chances for success.

At the same time, there are many affluent people in small communities who are not "professional" Angel Investors (but still meet the accreditation standards), but occasionally invest in a local business because they believe the investment is worthwhile, and they want to help their community.

These are the easiest types to work with because they usually take a passive role as an investor and might not require so much equity in your business.

For all others, be prepared to give up substantial equity in your company (maybe up to, or more than, 50%) and accept your new Investor as a board member — and quite often as a paid consultant as well.

One thing to watch out for is an aggressive personality, as they may tend to want to run your business for you.

Angel Investors will usually require you to consult with them before taking certain actions, like selling more stock or assets. They will also usually ask for anti-dilution protections to prevent you from selling stock at a lower price than they paid. This usually involves issuing more stock to the Investor to maintain their original equity ratio.

Finding Angel Investors

This process is quite a bit different than approaching lenders — although an Angel Investor could be both. Many Angels stay somewhat under the business radar, because they receive many more requests to look at deals than they could possibly be involved with.

Some networks claim they fund only 1% to 2% of the requests they receive.

This means you really need an introduction by a third party who knows both you and the investor. This eliminates a lot of wasted activity you would otherwise have to go through.

So, here is how I would suggest starting:

If your business is not a corporation, you will need to incorporate your business before seeking professional investors, because all outside professional investors will want shares of stock in your business when they invest. You can get information on incorporating your business at this website: http://bit.ly/dl3osm

Make sure your Business Plan is the best it can possibly be. This is your main selling tool, so it must be very well done to stand out above all the others an Angel Investor will receive.

If you need more information on creating a Business Plan, you can refer to my book, *"Small Business Planning: How to Plan Without Writing a Business Plan"* (available at Amazon.com and other booksellers).

Likewise, make sure your presentations (pitches) are up to date and polished — you only get one chance to make a first impression. Make it a good one.

Meet with members of your Advisory Board (you do have one, don't you?) and ask them if they have professional investor contacts they could introduce you to.

You should also meet with your banker early on, because a good banker should always have backup sources for money when the bank cannot be involved and they want to keep you as a customer.

A good banker should be able to introduce you to professional investors in your local area.

You definitely want to meet with your attorney, and accountant, as well as business colleagues and associates, to ask them if they could introduce you to any Angel Investors they know.

Again, this is where you need your various "pitches" polished and ready to go, because these contacts are not going to introduce you until they are convinced you know what you're doing and that you have your act together.

Although it is always better to have an introduction, or at least a referral, there are many other ways to find and make contact with professional investors directly. Here are a few:

Local University —

If you have a university with an entrepreneurship program near you — call the head of the program and make an appointment to meet with them. Usually such a person can refer you to an Angel Investor in the area with interests similar to yours.

Many universities also sponsor business incubators (there are over 1,200 in the U.S.) for many startups. You can get more information on incubators in the *Business Incubators* chapter of this book.

Chamber of Commerce—

You should contact your local *Chamber of Commerce* and inquire if they have investors who are members of the Chamber. Often these folks participate in this form of local business activity.

Small Business Development Center—

Most medium to large cities have a *Small Business Development Center*, and your local SBA or SCORE office should be able to direct you to the right person. Call them to see if they know of any Angel Investment groups in your area.

Angel Network—

You can search through a published list of Angel Investors in North America in the *Angel Network* at this address: http://www.angelnetwork.com/

AngelList—

This web-based Angel Investment group provides a listing of Angel Investors that indicate their preferred location and type of investment. The investors listed on this site are all professional investors, so be sure your inquiry is equally professional, and your Business Plan is "smashing." Take a look at https://angel.co/

Angel Capital Association —

Another Angel Directory is from the *Angel Capital Association*. This directory lists several hundred Angel Investors all across North America, by region. You can access this directory at the following Internet address: http://www.angelcapitalassociation.org/directory/

But remember, most Angels prefer to invest quite close to home. Often, the further away from home, the higher the expected rate of return on their investment, in order to make all the travel worth their time.

There is another avenue for finding Angel Investors, and that is through "paying" to get your business matched up with Investor interests. Usually the fee is quite modest, but I have not yet heard of very high success rates.

Here are a few of these services I am aware of:

Funding Post —

This is a service where you pay to list your company and what you need in the way of investment. Investors then periodically review the listings and contact the entrepreneur to discuss potential mutual interests. For more information, try this address: http://fundingpost.com

vFinance—

This platform is a repository of Angel Investors and Venture Capitalists, although I think there are better places to look for VCs. After you submit your requirements, you will need to pay for selected records of appropriate investors. The cost varies by just how wealthy you want your Angel Investor to be. For more information, use this address:
http://www.vfinance.com

Central Investment Network—

This is a platform that connects entrepreneurs in the central U.S. (Colorado, Kansas, Missouri, Montana, Utah, & Wyoming) with investors around the world.

They have a menu of costs to entrepreneurs, depending on the level of service and the amount of time you want to be listed in their database. For more information about this organization, go to this address:
http://www.centralinvestmentnetwork.com/

How Can I Get Rid of an Angel Investor?

As hard as it is to find an Angel Investor who will invest in your business, it is often more difficult to get rid of them if personalities clash, or the business does not perform as expected.

Obviously, your Angel intended to stay around until you executed your exit strategy, so they could reap their many-times return on their original investment.

However, many things can happen on the way to your exit strategy … you may have serious personal differences with your Angel … your company may not perform as expected, thus disappointing your Angel … your exit strategy may change as your company grows … you may need venture capital, which could dilute the ownership position of your Angel … or a host of other special reasons for wanting your Angel Investor out of your business.

NOTE: A professional investor will be aware of all of this and will usually want these issues covered in a contract that protects them in any of these events. You will need your attorney to approve the original contract for your protection.

Unless you can find someone (like a Venture Capitalist) to buy out your investor, and you can reach an amicable agreement with them, you are pretty much stuck with the person you select originally—at least until you execute your exit strategy, so … **CHOOSE CAREFULLY!**

The best time to address these issues is when writing the contract. Professional investors are aware of the pitfalls of investing in small startup businesses and therefore, often require a clearer exit strategy for themselves than just the exit strategy in your Business Plan.

Warning!

One warning about presenting your project to a "group" of investors at an "event." Some of these investor groups charge for the privilege of presenting to them. It may be all right to pay a few hundred dollars to attend a workshop or "boot camp" that they may recommend, but it is absolutely *NOT* necessary to pay to make a pitch to investors.

This practice has become more common recently, and, in my opinion, it is unethical and you do not want to become involved with anyone who charges in this manner.

There are plenty of good honest and ethical investors around—you don't need the shysters.

Finding an Angel Investor is usually not too difficult, but negotiating a deal with one can be more of a problem. Just remember to choose a new business partner carefully … don't jump on the first deal that is offered by an investor without thorough analysis by you and your advisors.

An Angel Investor may be with you for a very long time, so give it serious thought.

The granddaddy of all startup financing is *venture capital*. This is what most people think about when the term "startup" is mentioned. Unfortunately, venture capital is available to only a very small group of startups. But if you are in the high-tech, high-profit-potential world of startups — and have some progress to show a Venture Capitalist — this form of financing may be for you.

We'll discuss *Venture Capital* in the next chapter.

Chapter 5 —

Venture Capital

Whenever someone starts thinking about funding their new startup, they almost always think about venture capital funding — and that is usually a mistake! Venture capital is available to only a very few startups.

According to the *Kauffman Index of Entrepreneurial Activity*, about 6.5 million new full-time businesses are created each year. Of that number, less than 1,000 new startups (less than 4,000 overall) will receive venture capital funding.

A Venture Capitalist (VC) will only consider investing in startup businesses that have already been formed, and have proven their concept.

So, you can see that an entrepreneur's chance for attracting VC money is miniscule at best.

If your startup business is not potentially a fast growth, high-income-potential business — don't waste your time seeking venture capital ... especially from top tier VCs.

Here is what VCs are looking for:

> *They are interested in startups in the computer, biomedical, healthcare, media & entertainment, software, and most other*

types of high-tech industries. (There are some exceptions to this, but not many.)

Your business must have the potential for creating outstanding value to the investor through an eventual IPO, or a sale/merger — within 7 to 10 years.

You must have a strong, capable, and committed team of managers and technicians on board.

You must have a "proven" concept, whether product or service. VCs do not invest in "ideas" alone.

VCs will often look for opportunities where they can add value through their experience, connections, or future funding requirements.

They especially like to see a founder with strong leadership and business skills. It is even better if the founder has previously started a successful business in a similar field.

Remember, venture capital funding is not available for any entrepreneur in the very early or "proving" phase of their business. Most Venture Capitalists like to see others put up the first money, either by the founder(s) or an Angel Investor.

Even though some VCs occasionally offer up a little "seed" funding, they still like to see some proof of your business concept. In other words, venture capital funding likes to follow fast growth potential, big profits, and companies with an exit strategy for an IPO or a sale/merger. Businesses with smaller visions than that need not apply.

However, if you have a business in the early stages of a startup that meets the above criteria, then by all means, start looking for venture capital funding.

Additional VC Information

Here are three up-to-date sources of information on venture capital — which firms are investing and where they are investing:

MoneyTree Report—

The most up-to-date information available on venture capital comes from the PriceWaterhouseCoopers *MoneyTree report*. This report tells which VC is currently making investments, and in what industries. It gives the most up-to-date information on VC activity. To access this report, go to https://www.pwcmoneytree.com

National Venture Capital Association—

This is another excellent source of information regarding equity funding. It provides extensive information on the Venture Capital industry. To visit the website, go to this Internet address: http://www.nvca.org

Community Development Venture Capitalists (CDIC) —

Many VCs are now looking for investment opportunities in more "rural" areas of mid-America. They have come to realize that ideas hatched in a small town diner can be just as good as ideas hatched in Silicon Valley or Boston.

However, don't think the VCs are relaxing their requirements just to tap into this large pool of talented entrepreneurs in small-town America — you still need to have a high quality Business Plan and presentation.

If you are located somewhere in "rural" America and are trying to start or expand your business, you can get some more information on this form of venture capital by contacting the *Community Development Venture Capital Alliance* at http://cdvca.org/

A Word on Venture Capital

In the event you do need to seek venture capital for a high profit potential business, there are a couple of key issues you need to remember:

Introductions —

Large VC firms do not read business plans that come in "over the transom." You need a personal introduction, or at least a referral, before you will be taken seriously.

It is also extremely important that you contact a specific person within your chosen VC firm. Each person in the firm usually specializes in one of the areas the firm invests in, and you need to get your business plan into the hands of the person specializing in your industry. This is another reason that introductions are so important.

Preparation —

You must be prepared with your "pitch", your "Executive Summary," and your "Business Plan." These three things must represent your absolute best effort if you want to make a positive connection with a VC.

You also must be ready to give a presentation at any time. If you and your advisors are actively searching for an interested Venture Capitalist, you never know when you might get a call to go and make a presentation.

* * * * *

Use your advisors (that's why you need a strong group of advisors). Work the Internet. Use your network of contacts. Join your city's VC association if one is available — but get that personal introduction to your selected VC.

Up to now we have looked at bank financing, SBA loans, Angel Investors, and mainstream Venture Capital. But there is another avenue for Venture/Angel funding that is extremely popular because it also includes substantial help and guidance in getting a business started. It is called a *Business Incubator,* and is discussed in more detail in the next chapter.

Chapter 6 —

Business Incubators

If you don't think that your business is ready for an Angel Investor or Venture Capital, perhaps you could better benefit from working with a *Business Incubator* to get your company shaped up and ready for outside investors.

A Business Incubator is not everyone's cup of tea, but if you are thinking of starting up a high-tech business, or some very specialized product or service in a narrow niche, you may want to consider applying to a business incubator operator for start up assistance.

Business incubators have been around the U.S. since 1959. They all operate a little differently, but basically they offer space to work, technical and entrepreneurial advice and mentoring, and in some cases, a small stipend of "seed" money to help get your business started.

There are about 1,200 incubators in the U.S. and several thousand more around the world, including developing countries.

Most of the incubators themselves are nonprofits, and are usually supported by local government (cities and counties) and universities. There are also a few for-profit organizations that also promote the incubator concept — but typically with more intensity.

Following are descriptions of the four major types of incubator programs currently available:

The Standard Incubator Program

This is a fee-based program where participants receive office space, computer and basic office equipment, and access to expert mentors in their field.

The cost can range from a few hundred dollars per month to a few thousand, and it is usually expected that participants will grow and expand to their own facilities within three to five years.

The University Program

This program is usually directed at students of the University, and the participant is expected to expand to their own facilities upon graduation from the University, although some universities offer programs for alumni.

Unlike the Standard program, this program is typically free, and some universities offer grants to the entrepreneur to help them get started.

Services provided are similar to the *Standard Program* in providing space, access to facilities, and assistance from experienced staff and mentors.

The Niche Program

This program is more specialized in that it caters to businesses that are highly specialized, like food or environmental products. This program is especially beneficial to first-time entrepreneurs requiring specialized instruction, or companies that require access to specialized equipment.

This program is also fee-based, although some of the facilities will take an equity stake in the business.

The Accelerator Program

This program is intended for fast-growth companies that want to attract investors.

Most of the accelerator programs are run by groups of successful business owners and investors. This type of program takes a percentage equity stake in your business, but also provides seed money to get started. They also provide a facility for your business, and access to necessary equipment and guidance from mentors.

Accelerator programs are usually more intense and shorter in duration (about 90 days). The focus on this program is to quickly get your business in a position to attract the interest of investors.

Probably the best-known accelerator programs talked about today are "Y Combinator" and "TechStars." Y Combinator takes on a variety of company types, while TechStars concentrates on technology companies.

Currently, Y Combinator is reducing the size of their twice-yearly accelerator classes, from 80+ companies, to less than 50. They are also reducing by about 50% the amount of investment money most companies receive upon graduation from the class. You can get more information on Y Combinator at this URL: http://ycombinator.com/atyc.html

TechStars is similar to Y Combinator, but they concentrate on high-tech companies (with a few exceptions). They offer one class per year at their 4 primary locations, plus several programs with corporate partners like Microsoft, Nike, etc. For more information on TechStars programs, visit this URL http://www.techstars.com/program/faqs/

There are other accelerator programs currently in operation, plus some that come and go, so do your research and see if you can find a program that best suits your particular business.

* * * * *

All Incubator programs offer the participants a great opportunity to better define their business and create a Business Plan and pitch that can attract venture capital.

Unfortunately, there are many more applicants than spaces available, so the application process can be quite daunting.

For an incubator in your area of interest, you can search the website of the *National Business Incubation Association*. Their URL is:
http://www.nbia.org/links_to_member_incubators/

The forms of financing a business we have looked at so far are available to only a small portion of the 6.5 million businesses that will start up this year. So, in the next chapter, let's look at one of the newer forms of business financing — *Peer-to-Peer Lending*.

Chapter 7 —

Peer-to-peer Lending

This form of business financing has become more popular the last few years. It allows you to borrow a modest amount online — usually up to about $50,000 (although it can go higher) — from a willing private lender (or multiple lenders) by going through a brokerage service.

The terms of the loan can be surprisingly low, depending on your credit score and the program you use, but you don't always need to have a real high credit score to participate.

Generally speaking, you post your money requirements online at a brokers website, and ask for a loan to cover your need. Lenders will then review your business submission and decide if they want to loan money for your expressed use, and at what terms. Each broker works a little differently, but that is basically the idea of Peer-to-peer lending.

In a few cases, an accredited investor (Angel) may like your ideas and business model so well they will contact you directly about investing in your business instead of just lending you money. You probably shouldn't count on this however.

There are lenders and brokers regularly entering and leaving this type of small business financing, but here are some websites for the more popular Peer-to-Peer Lenders today:

Prosper —

Prosper claims to be the largest peer-to-peer lender in the world, with 1,120,000 people involved in their program. The process is straightforward and easy for anyone to do — just make sure your pitch (custom loan listing) follows their guidelines and is the best you can provide — this is where you "sell" your project. You can access their website at this address: http://www.prosper.com/

Peer Lending Network —

The Peer Lending Network is an affiliate of Prosper.com, but works a little differently. Instead of interest rates being set by PLN, people looking for a loan post a listing for a peer loan with the amount they need at a rate they can afford, and lenders bid on the listings by bidding the amount and rate they are willing to lend the borrower. More information is available at this address:
http://www.peerlendingnetwork.com/index.html

Lending Club —

Lending Club has about 32,000 borrowers and around 50,000 individual investors in their program. They have surpassed $325 million in loan originations with an average loan size of about $10,000. For more information on the Lending Club, go to this address: http://www.lendingclub.com/kb/index.php?View=entry& EntryID=94

GoBig Network —

This lender operates similarly to the other peer-to-peer lenders, except they deal in much larger investment amounts, and appeal to larger investment firms. That also means you will need a very professional "Business Plan," because you are asking for larger investments from professional investors. For more information on this company go to this address: http://www.gobignetwork.com/

Zopa —

Zopa was the world's first peer-to-peer lending company when it launched in the UK in 2005. Most p2p companies since then have emulated Zopa's platform.

Unfortunately, Zopa does not currently operate in the U.S. and can only be used by those who are residents of the United Kingdom. To find out more about the UK service, go to this address: http://uk.zopa.com/?utm_expid=2529841-21

MicroVentures —

This company operates a little differently than any of the others in that it functions more like an Investment Bank. They are looking for investment opportunities in the $100,000 to $500,000 range.

You should be aware that this group is looking at the same industries as regular Angel Investors and Venture Capitalists. In fact, most of the investors involved are Angel Investors.

You begin by filling out an application and submitting it, along with your business plan, and $100, to the company.

Your application will then be assigned to someone in the organization who will analyze your application and determine if it meets all the necessary requirements to be posted on their website. If approved initially, you will be asked for another $250 for a more in-depth analysis of your business plan.

If their in-depth analysis of your business plan determine that your business is suitable for listing on their platform, MicroVentures will complete the necessary documents and then list your opportunity on their website.

Investors will then review your business and determine if they are interested in your business. You will then (hopefully) receive one, or many; investment offers to fund your business.

This works like a combination of peer-to-peer lending, crowdfunding, and Angel Investing—all overseen by an investment banker ... who will charge a 10% commission, plus offering "expenses."

Here is the contact information for MicroVentures:
http://www.microventures.com/

* * * *

If your business, or project, and financial need are small enough, you might be interested in the currently popular form of raising money—*Crowdfunding*. This concept of financing a business is discussed in the following chapter.

Chapter 8 —

Crowdfunding

Crowdfunding is a concept in flux. The original concept of this type of small business financing consisted of posting information about your business, or "project," on one of the websites specializing in crowdfunding, and asking for "donations" in exchange for simple "rewards," or minor gifts.

The original (and still current) concept did not allow "investments" or any expectations of monetary returns. Any money contributed to the project was strictly a "donation."

This is still an excellent source of financing a specific "project," but doesn't always work well if trying to start a new business.

If you have an interest in financing a project, especially a creative, ecological, or human-interest type of project, I have provided some information on the more popular crowdfunding websites later in this chapter.

IMPORTANT NOTE: *There are major changes about to take place with the entire concept of crowdfunding. There is a section in the recently passed law,* Jumpstart Our Business Startups (JOBS) Act, *which was passed on April 5, 2012, and then handed over to the U.S. Securities and Exchange Commission (SEC) to write the guiding regulations.*

Unfortunately, the SEC is a giant bureaucracy that is years behind in its work, and all the deadlines for implementing the crowdfunding section of the act have passed with no progress shown.

There are over a hundred new crowdfunding sites gearing up to launch as soon as the SEC completes the regulations and gives the go-ahead. When this might happen is anyone's guess.

Investors

At the same time, be aware that individuals who are "accredited investors" can always invest in your business, if that is what you are searching for. There is always a possibility that one of these investors will see your information on a crowdfunding site and contact you directly expressing an interest in investing—but don't count on it.

Meanwhile

While waiting for the new regulations there are some things you can do if you have a particular project in mind, and have developed a simple presentation describing it. You should present it on one of the existing crowfunding websites, and ask for donations to your project.

Although new crowdfunding sites will be launching on a regular basis, here is information on the more popular websites currently set up for *Crowdfunding*:

Kickstarter —

Kickstarter claims to be the largest funding platform for *creative projects* in the world. They specialize in raising money for a variety of projects from the worlds of music, film, art, technology, design, food, publishing and other creative fields. They have raised around $372,000 million to date, with a success rate for applicants of about 44%. For more information, go to this URL: http://kck.st/Pvd2Pv

Peerbackers —

This platform is a little different from some of the other crowdfunding platforms in that if you do not meet your target pledge amount, you can still take whatever money has been pledged, **IF** you can deliver the rewards you promised in your post. Otherwise, the monies are returned to the contributors. For more information on this company, go to this website: http://bit.ly/y4ncAg

GoFundMe —

This source is one of the earliest crowdfunding websites for individuals. The site's name was changed from "Create-a-Fund" to "GoFundMe" in 2010, and proclaims that it is the funding source for "everything else" — including starting a business. It offers opportunities to fund a wide array of different needs and causes, and claims the site is growing at 20% per month. *Fast Company* magazine says this about it: "It's a place where family, friends, and communities, come together to support one another." For more information, you can check out their website at: http://bit.ly/J4L6gn

indiegogo —

This website makes the claim that they have over 60,000 people raising million of dollars in over 200 countries worldwide through their website. This site raises money for a very large variety of uses, and seems to also raise higher amounts for larger projects — including starting a new business. For more information, go to this website: http://bit.ly/RfjGvN

Rock The Post —

This is a fairly new crowdfunding site that works similar to the sites above, except they also offer help to new entrepreneurs to make their posting more attractive to donors or investors. For more information, go to this website: http://www.rockthepost.com/

Quirky —

This is a crowdfunding site directed specifically at Inventors. It was started in 2009 and brings about 3 new products per week to market. The big attraction at this site is that they have partnerships with many big-box retail stores where your developed invention could be sold. Check out this site at http://www.quirky.com

WeFunder—

This site specializes in startups and claims to help new businesses work through the maze of government regulations governing raising money. They helped push the JOBS Act through Congress, and are now set up to accept small investments as soon as the SEC releases their regulations. In the meantime, investors must still be "accredited" investors. You can take a look at this concept at https://wefunder.com

Crowdfunder—

This site is a typical crowdfunding site with a heavy emphasis on social projects. *Crowdfunder* was also heavily involved in the passage of the JOBS Act, and is fully geared up to allow small investors to participate—as soon as the SEC releases the regulations. You can get all the details for this website at http://www.crowdfunder.com

* * * * *

There are other crowdfunding sites floating around the Internet, with many more (over 100 at last count) coming, but those above seem to be the most popular today. Keep in mind that as we get closer to the SEC releasing their regulations, there will be other new sites jumping the gun by temporarily setting up a traditional "donations-only" site, or a site for "accredited" investors only, which they can quickly change when the SEC regulations are released.

Updating

In the meantime, while waiting for the SEC to act, if you would like to keep informed on the progress of the new crowdfunding regulations, take a look at the posts on my blog from time to time: http://bizmaverickblog.com — Click on the Category *Business Funding*.

We have been discussing some of the more common methods of financing a small business, but now let us start looking at more *Creative Business Financing*, starting with the next chapter.

Chapter 9 —

Creative Business Financing

Well, if you have tried all the avenues of financing your new business that have been discussed in prior chapters — and have been unsuccessful so far — don't worry, because there is still a variety of business financing possibilities yet to be tried.

"Creative," or "alternative," business financing is usually not a normal place to search for startup, or operating, money, but take a look at the financing sources described in the following and see if this type of business financing may be the answer to your needs.

Customers

This may seem an unlikely source of business financing, but it is much more common than you might think. Following is an actual case history of my own about how this can work:

> *I had a customer come to my company and ask if we could develop some special tooling to be used by them in their manufacturing process … there was nothing similar available in their industry at the time. This customer advanced the cost of development and prototyping in exchange for a 6-month exclusive right to the product after we began manufacturing the tooling.*

The prototypes were successful; we patented the tooling concept, and set up a new special manufacturing department – paid for by the customer we had the agreement with.

After the 6-month exclusive agreement expired, we formed a new spin-off company, expanded our sales effort worldwide, and the new company became highly successful ... with the business startup cost paid for by the original customer.

The key to customer financing is to have something they want and need, and then simply asking them how they can participate in the upfront financing of fulfilling that need.

It's a little more difficult before you actually start your business, but if your new business could fulfill a strong need, you still might be able to put a deal together.

Vendors

This form of creative business financing is common if you are just looking for extended terms on something you are buying, or need to buy, from vendors, such as: inventory of parts or products.

But, if you are developing a new product or service you also may be able to obtain some development financing from a vendor who stands to gain substantially when your product goes to market.

This can be done as a loan, which is the simplest way, or you can pledge stock against the advance — or any of several similar scenarios. When you have two willing businesses, there is always some way to make creative business financing work.

Just ask, because this is not something vendors will usually seek you out for.

Employees

If your business currently has employees, and you need money for expansion or new product development, you might be able to joint venture with your employees to finance the startup costs.

The potential rewards need to be substantial however, because employees are not entrepreneurs, and they rarely have extra money to spare.

So, if you do joint venture with your employees, make it real — this cannot be just a token attempt, or you will lose the trust and respect of your current employees plus everyone who comes to work for you in the future.

Leasing vs. Buying

If your new business requires equipment, furniture, or fixtures, something you should strongly consider is leasing rather than buying. There are numerous advantages in leasing, not the least of which is the preservation of cash.

Often, the equipment vendor can provide an attractive leasing program, or there are third-party companies that will buy the equipment and lease it back to you. Be sure to do a thorough economic analysis before you make any commitments however.

Hard-Money Lenders

This should be just about your last-ditch effort at creative business financing. Hard-money loans are aptly named because the lender is usually a private individual, or small group of individuals who loan on sure things, charge exorbitant fees and interest, require substantial collateral, and want their money repaid fairly quickly.

This form of financing is not usually appropriate for financing startups, but it can be highly valuable if you only need a short-term bridge loan for your business expansion, or new product release. Just be sure you do your research thoroughly and know whom you are dealing with — sometimes there is a fine line between an honest hard-money lender, and a shyster.

To find a hard-money lender in your area, I recommend you work through your banker or advisory group.

Factoring

If you have already started your business and are selling your product(s) or service on terms, you can quickly "sell' your invoices to a "factoring" company to get immediate cash instead of waiting for the customers to pay.

Just be aware that factoring companies charge exorbitantly high fees, so this too should be one of your last resorts for money.

Community

This is different from the *Community Development Agency* concept, and is a rare form of creative business financing, but it can happen. In cases where an entire community wants you to start your business there — or keep your existing business from moving away, the community can come up with several different incentives.

The most typical is a reduction, or postponement, of various taxes normally paid to the community. Occasionally, however, financial investments are also made. Or, land or a building that is owned by the community are offered to the business as an incentive to build in the community

Community financial assistance requires a great deal of research and negotiation if you are just starting up, and you also might have the entire community looking over your shoulder as you set up and run your business. Work through your banker, advisory board, business development agency, or a city council member who publicly supports new businesses in your community. They should certainly be able to refer you to the right people to talk to.

> **Note:** *A recent development is that a very few cities are now directly providing Venture Capital for new business startups. This is a real long shot and only for businesses with high employment potential. However, it might be worthwhile to check with your own city to see if they have such a program.*

Think Incrementally

This is a pretty old-fashioned way to start a business, but there have probably been more successful businesses started this way than by any other. By "think incrementally," I am referring to the entrepreneur who has a big dream, but little money, so they start a small — possibly unrelated — business, build it up to profitability and then sells it.

The entrepreneur then uses that money to start another small business ... and repeats the process as many times as necessary until they have the money to start their dream business.

Not only will this approach give you the money to start your dream business, but a couple of small business successes will go a long way with future partners, investors or Venture Capitalists.

Other Sources

Here are a few other possibilities for creative business financing. It will take some digging around to see what is available in your area, but it may be well worth it:

Grants (from businesses and foundations). Government grants are generally not available for starting a for-profit business (with a very few exceptions).

Economic Development Centers. Most cities have a form of assistance for small businesses – but not always direct financial assistance. Your Advisors should be able to direct you. You should also contact your Chamber of Commerce, or City Clerk's office for information on a center in your area.

Small Business Development Centers. Similar to the Economic Development Centers, but with somewhat different goals and programs. Check with your Advisory group, they should be able to introduce you to the right contacts. If they can't help you, contact your local Chamber of Commerce, or City Clerk's office … and fire your group of advisors.

Prizes for business plan competitions. Search the Internet for current competitions with monetary payouts.

Well, there you have a few creative business financing methods to consider. When your business cannot raise money through more conventional channels, creative business financing may be your best alternative.

This also means, however, that you will have to be even better prepared than with conventional financing, and you will likely need to prepare a different kind of Business Plan for each source of financing (depending on their requirements).

Actually, most of the financing methods previously discussed apply to very specific situations—and the majority of small businesses do not fit those situations.

So, in the next chapter we'll discuss the most common means of small business financing—*Owner Financing.*

Chapter 10—

Owner Financing

I hate to tell you this, but owner financing is the most common method for financing startups, especially smaller businesses that pose little interest for Angel investors and Venture Capitalists.

The vast majority of small business startups are owner financed, and it is most likely that you will need to finance your own startup this way as well.

Where will you get the money?

That's where this chapter on owner financing comes in, and here are the typical activities that most entrepreneurs turn to for gathering in the money they need to finance their new business.

Your Own Savings

Many people save for years just to someday start their own business. This is the ideal situation. However, if you haven't done that, maybe you have a 401k, an IRA, or a stock portfolio you can cash in for your new business financing.

Yes, you may have to pay taxes and penalties, but at least you may get your business started.

Of course, you are also betting your future on your ability to build a thriving business. If you wipe out your savings and retirement portfolio, you are casting yourself adrift to rebuild for the future.

Signature Loan

This used to be a common source for obtaining a small amount of money to be used in an owner's business. You only needed to have a strong personal financial statement, a good credit score, and a good positive relationship with your bank ... but not today.

This type of loan is more difficult to get right now, but times will likely change and this form of lending may eventually come back.

Just remember that the bank is not your Angel Investor ... they are making this type of loan to you personally, on your word and your reputation.

Home Equity Loan

In the past, when banks would loan up to 150% of the value of your home (and most homes where overvalued), this was one of the most common forms of raising cash.

Now, it is much more difficult to get a home equity loan at all unless you have substantial equity in your home (at current values), plus a good reputation with your bank—including a very high credit score.

You also need to think about what you are risking here, and if you have a family, they need to be part of this decision.

Personal Asset Loan

If you own anything of value, such as; a vacation cabin, motorcycle, boat, car, real estate, and the like, you may be able to borrow money using any of these personal assets as collateral—maybe.

Selling Personal Assets

If you own personal assets, per the above, and cannot borrow against them, you could consider selling them. If you are not using many of these assets, this may be a better avenue than borrowing against them, because it will make your business balance sheet that much stronger.

Credit Cards

Many new businesses have been started on the strength of the founder's credit cards. I never recommend an entrepreneur use their personal credit cards for starting or running their business, so just know that this is a risky gamble, and that you will be personally liable for the debt.

But, if you believe the gamble is one you and your family are willing to take—it could be a source of startup funding for your new business.

Taking on a Partner

Unless you have been working with a partner from the very beginning, or your plans call for taking on a known partner, you can run into all kinds of problems when taking on a partner just to get financing for your business.

This is especially true for the smaller small business. A partner is different than an investor in that a typical partner will definitely want to run the business with you ... and often this does not work out in a very small business.

Keeping Your Day Job

You may want to keep your regular job and continue your pre-venture planning while you save up as much money as possible to start a business.

If your business involves developing a prototype or doing extensive market testing, you may be able to keep your regular job while you work on the preliminary aspects of your business.

The major problem with this method of owner financing is that all too many people use "lack of startup money" as an excuse to stay in a job they don't like and NEVER get around to starting their own business — don't be one of those!

Borrowing from Family and Friends

There have probably been more new businesses started by borrowing money from family and friends than by any other single method. With rare exception, most "smaller" (owner/operator) small businesses are started by owner financing — and "family and friends" is where that financing often comes from.

One warning however: Make very sure of your plans and calculations for your business, because you could end up with no friends and no family (that are speaking to you).

Not having money to finance your business is not a good reason for not getting started. If you have done your homework properly, so you are quite certain your business idea is viable, and you have the proper passion (obsession?) for the business, there should be nothing stopping you from reaching your dreams.

There is one form of business financing we have not addressed yet — *Bootstrapping!* I've left this until last because true bootstrapping is the most difficult method of financing your new business. Let's look at it in the next chapter.

Chapter 11—

Bootstrapping

Well, now we get to the heart of the matter—financing your business the most difficult way of all by *Bootstrapping!*

Bootstrapping is usually the last thing anyone thinks about when they start planning their new business. In fact, it is nearly impossible to plan this type of financing, because it functions in a very unstructured manner.

The common definition of bootstrapping is really quite simple: "Grow your business by putting everything you make back into your business—and never spend more than you make."

That's all well and good if you have a business that is already started, and you don't want to grow any faster than your business can self-fund itself.

But what if you don't have a business started yet ... or don't have any money to start a business ... or don't have any assets ... or don't have any credit available ... or don't have any friends or family that can provide some startup financing—can you still start a business using the concept of "bootstrapping?"

Yes, you certainly can — it's just going to be a little harder, and it will likely take longer. Of course, it can only be done if you have the basic traits of an entrepreneur, like: passion, commitment, and willingness to have the business be your life for the foreseeable future.

These are the characteristics that most average people do not have, they are found only in those who are endowed with a true entrepreneurial spirit.

I'm going to discuss the concept of absolute bootstrapping (creating a business from nothing) by presenting a story about *Jane — the Entrepreneur*, and how she used bootstrapping to build her business.

Although Jane is fictional, her story is being played out everyday all around the world. It could be your story as well.

The Story of Jane — A True Entrepreneur

Let's go back to just before the Great Recession of 2007, when Jane worked at a job she hated, but needed her paycheck to live on, which means she lived from paycheck to paycheck (just like many of us).

Although she thought a lot about wanting to take control of her life and starting a business of her own, Jane never had any money left over from her paycheck to put aside for starting a business.

Then one-day Jane's boss called her into his office and informed her that he was closing down her entire department, and her services were no longer needed.

Note: *if you want to know what this feels like, take a look at the short video at this website:* http://bit.ly/9gB4ZB *(scroll down that page a ways).*

Knowing her talent had always been in demand in the past, Jane started sending out resumes and filling out applications — all to no avail. It seemed that just about all companies and businesses were laying people off instead of hiring.

Eventually, Jane lost most of her material possessions ... her house was gone ... she sold her furniture to buy food ... she traded her car for an older van ... and moved in with her sister's family.

Jane was now jobless, homeless, broke, and with little hope for the future.

But, like many of us, Jane had always wanted to do something that she thought "mattered." She had always had a desire to have more control over her life and work for herself instead of some faceless large corporation.

The problem was — Jane was broke — she had no money to start any kind of business, and her credit was now practically non-existent.

Still, Jane had always fantasized about owning a little neighborhood coffee shop. She was a "people person," and wanted a business where she could interact with people and make a modest living at the same time.

Jane's Dream

Jane began to think more and more about how she might be able to achieve her dream of one-day owning a coffee shop.

She went to the City Clerk's office and researched what it would take to acquire various licenses and permits to start a coffee business. She learned all the rules and regulations involved.

She started to keep a *Planning Workbook* where she could record all the information she collected and all the plans she made.

Next, Jane visited a variety of coffee shops, carts, and kiosks around town and started conversations about how they got started. (That's one of the things about entrepreneurs — they like to help others also get their business started.)

With some basic knowledge, Jane then began to research the cost of equipment, space costs, who the product suppliers were, manpower requirements — she even attended a Community College adult education class on starting and running a small business.

She sat in various coffee shops and counted customers. She hung out at coffee kiosks in large building lobbies and counted customers — she even chatted with some of the customers to get an idea of why they bought their coffee at that particular spot.

Jane next searched around town to determine where there were gaps in coffee sources ... where people would have to go some distance to buy a cup of coffee.

Although the more research she did, and the more confident she became that she could start a coffee business in the right place, the more she realized she would never be able to raise the money to start her business.

Broke, unemployed, homeless and living with her sister's family — and having a credit score that was below low — the future was pretty bleak.

This is where the girls and boys are separated from the women and men — where those who can ... do, and those who can't ... stay stuck where they are indefinitely.

With enough thought and determination, any person can rise above their current situation and achieve the life they dream about. That's when Jane began to form her actual PLAN!

NOTE: For details on how Jane used her "Planning Workbook," go to another book in my *Primer Series*, titled *Small Business Planning: How to Plan Without Writing a Business Plan.* Available at Amazon.com and other booksellers.

Jane's Plan

Jane had amassed a large amount of information about selling coffee and had it all recorded in her *Planning Workbook.* All she needed was money to put her plans into effect.

Or.......

Why not break her plans down into smaller increments, or stages, and implement each stage as she made money from the prior stage. This is truly basic "bootstrapping" — *taking a small trickle of income from any source, and using that money to pull the business up by its "bootstraps" to continuously build upon that trickle until the ideal business is operating.*

Sure, it would take Jane a lot longer to achieve her goal of operating a neighborhood coffee shop, but she was sure she could do it.

So, Jane sold the last of her personal possessions on *Craigslist* and went to the City offices and paid for her licenses and permits to operate as a sidewalk vendor in permitted areas.

She then went to thrift stores and a restaurant supply store to buy a small folding table, a tablecloth, a couple of thermos pots, and some paper coffee cups and lids.

Jane went to one of the coffee houses she had spent time in during her market research, and made arrangements to buy bulk coffee for her thermoses at a greatly reduced price.

Now she was ready for her first day of business.

Day One!

In Jane's planning, she set up guidelines for how she was going to run her business. Her guidelines looked something like this:

I will not deliberately break any rules, regulations, or laws.

I will not become a nuisance by impeding the flow of traffic.

I will be professional in dealing with customers (remember, they are probably grumpy because they haven't had their morning coffee yet — I am there to fulfill that need).

I will use only the highest quality coffee I can find (most large gourmet coffee shops sell their coffee in bulk for parties and events.)

I will keep my area and myself extremely neat and clean. I am not looking for charity ... I am starting a business, and I am a professional businessperson — an entrepreneur.

I will not compete with my source for coffee.

I will brand myself as someone "special" in the coffee vendor world of my city.

Most important, in the words of Winston Churchill, I will: "Never, never, never, give up."

On her first day, Jane filled her thermoses with coffee from the coffee shop owned by her new friend she had made while studying coffee shops. Then took her other equipment, and went to an area she had previously studied, and set up her folding table before the early morning rush.

She had made a small sign to put on her table announcing her new service, "*Java On The Fly!*" She had also hand printed some small cards that said "Good For One Free Cup of Coffee On (*next days date*)." She would hand these out on her first day to anyone who bought a cup of coffee from her — hoping to encourage them to come back again tomorrow. This was phase one of her loyalty-building program.

Jane took in less than $20 that first day, and after she paid for tomorrow morning's coffee, she would have very little left. But, she was ecstatic, because with her first customer she became a legitimate business — she was now truly an entrepreneur.

The Long View

It was a tough few months for Jane. On weekends when the downtown offices were closed, she would go to sporting events and set up in the parking lot. Or, she would go to kid's soccer games and little league games and set up near the field entrance. On warm days she would add cold drinks to her menu.

Sometimes she would set up outside a theater just as people were leaving. Or at the exit doors to any major event that was in town.

If she was asked to leave any of these locations, she would go somewhere else and set up — after all, she was "mobile" at this point.

Jane's marketing became ever more creative as she became the city's "mystery" coffee person. She gave free coffee to anyone who accurately guessed where she would be located next weekend … and on and on. She just kept adding ideas to the "Marketing" section of her *Planning Workbook*.

She coveted cash and added to her "business fund" every day. Some days not much — but other days more than you might guess. She made sure that her few bills were paid on time, and gradually started to rebuild her credit standing.

Jane also continued to study and learn all she could about business and coffee. She experimented with making coffee at her sister's and filling her thermoses. She even tried her hand at roasting samples of coffee beans in order to understand the process and nuances of coffee roasting.

Jane Steps Up

Then one day Jane got a call from one of her friends in the coffee business telling her about a Kiosk Coffee Cart that was becoming available for sale.

The seller was going out of business — the work was just too hard — and he wanted to sell all his equipment as quickly as possible.

Jane used most of her business fund to make a down payment on the Kiosk Coffee Cart and arranged to make payments to the owner until it was paid off.

Jane had previously noticed that one of the large office buildings had a large, nearly empty, lobby, so she visited the building management company and made a well thought out pitch to put a very professional looking Kiosk Coffee Cart in the building's lobby.

The building management people had been looking for someone to provide coffee in the lobby, but they wanted someone they could be confident would stick with the business.

Since they had all seen Jane's street vendor business and were impressed with her business acumen and dedication, they gave her very attractive terms for setting up her new coffee Kiosk in the lobby of their building.

One of the building management's requirements was that she must have liability insurance on her operation that would protect the building owners and the management company.

So Jane searched for an insurance agent that would set her up with adequate — and affordable — liability insurance for her business. It took patience and perseverance, but she finally got the insurance she needed.

She operated her Kiosk in the building lobby during the week and still ran her "mobile" operation at local events on the weekends. Now, her business fund was growing more rapidly and she quickly paid off her Kiosk coffee cart.

Jane's Advisory Board

Another one of her coffee shop colleagues called one day to tell her about another Kiosk Coffee Cart she knew of for sale, and if Jane wanted to expand, this would be a great opportunity.

This possibility wasn't in Jane's *Planning Workbook*, and she wondered what she should do. So, she went to see a person she knew at the bank where she had her account and asked them if they knew of anyone who would become a volunteer member of her "Advisory Board."

The banker was delighted to be an advisor to Jane and her business—he knew that as the business grew his bank would benefit. He also said he had a friend who was a successful businessman in town who occasionally sat on Advisory Boards, and he would ask him to join Jane's group as well.

Jane also knew she was approaching the point where she should be getting some help with her bookkeeping, so she asked the banker for a recommendation for an accountant.

She not only arranged for some bookkeeping and accounting work to be done, but also asked the accountant to serve on her Advisory Board.

The accountant was happy to serve, and Jane was now a small part of the city's business network.

One day, Jane asked a friend to run her coffee cart for her during a lunch period while she catered a light lunch for her new Advisory Board in one of the communal conference rooms in the building where she had her Coffee Cart business.

This was where she described how she had started her business and what she had accomplished to date. Then she explained her potential opportunity to expand her Kiosk Coffee Cart business by buying another coffee cart and setting it up in another high-traffic area she had previously identified.

This did not fit with her early business planning, and she needed advice on what to do at this point. This was why she had formed her Advisory Board — to have someone to bounce new ideas off of.

The Advisors pointed out that one of the main reasons for Jane's success was her personal attention to the business and especially to her customers. Jane not only sold coffee, but she was quick with verbal pats on the back for the good times, and a shoulder to lean on during troubled times. She was always there, and always a delight to see. Jane *was* her business.

This type of operation is very difficult to duplicate early in a business's growth. The advisors did not believe an employee would pull off the same success in a second location, and they felt this was not yet the time to take on a business "partner."

But they did come up with an idea. They suggested that Jane buy the second coffee cart, and then find someone (preferably someone she knew) who was looking to start a business. Then try to arrange for them to operate the second Kiosk Coffee Cart on a "shared" basis … they could run it as if they owned it (under Jane's general guidance), and pay Jane a portion of the proceeds.

This would allow Jane to pay off her second coffee cart, and at the same time provide an opportunity for some aspiring entrepreneur to start bootstrapping their own business by building up their own startup fund.

Under this concept the hardest part, obviously, is finding the right person to run the additional location. In addition, it meant that Jane would be spread thin training the new "owner" and making sure that her standards for customer service and adherence to her guidelines were being followed.

There were a few stumbling blocks along the way, but basically, it worked so well that Jane bought a third coffee cart and established another person in bootstrapping their business dreams.

But, after setting up two additional Kiosk Coffee Carts, Jane was at another crossroads in her business. So, she again turned to her Advisory Board for input on what they thought about her next potential move.

Jane's Dream Is In Sight

If you remember, Jane's dream was to own a neighborhood coffee shop; so she emphasized this to her Advisory Group and asked if they thought she was on the right track, and what step they thought she should take next.

Because of her passion, acquired business acumen, and the incredible hard work she had put into her business, the group came up with the suggestion that she sell her Kiosk businesses outright, preferably to the current operators, and concentrate on creating her coffee house.

Jane had always kept her eye out for just the right place to establish her coffee house, and knew exactly where she wanted to start it. It was the sudden availability of this particular location that precipitated the crossroads she was now facing.

Opening up a retail shop of any kind takes a lot of planning, hard work—and money. Jane had some money from her "business fund," some additional coming in from her sale of the Kiosk Coffee Carts, but lacked quite a bit to complete the shop.

Her credit rating was now much improved, but she was still not "bankable." She had "bootstrapped" her way from nothing to the threshold of achieving her dream—but she was not there yet.

This was also the point where her Advisory Board recommended she incorporate her business ... so she became *Java On The Fly, Inc.* It was then that the successful businessman who was on her Advisory Board stepped up and invested in her new corporation, with a clause allowing her to buy back the shares of stock based on a formula to determine stock value at that time, plus any other fees agreed upon.

Jane's "End" Game

Well, needless to say that Jane completed creation of her neighborhood coffee shop and it was a smashing success. She had bootstrapped her business all along the way until she caught the eye of an investor, with her passion and hard work.

She had long since moved out of her sister's house and bought a small uptown Condo. All her bills were paid—she even took a fair salary from the business. Jane was totally suited to this kind of business and everything was running like clockwork.

So, is that the end of the story?

It certainly could be, since Jane had achieved her original dream of owning a small neighborhood coffee shop. That's all she had ever wanted for as long as she could remember — and now she had it.

But … in keeping with the theme of bootstrapping, let's look at "The Rest of The Story."

Between the time Jane first wrote her dream down in her *Planning Workbook*, until this point, something happened to her — she became a full-fledged entrepreneur.

Jane was no longer content to just serve coffee and pastries to neighborhood traffic. She had the entrepreneurial itch, that once contracted can never be cured.

That's when Jane started to vertically integrate by renting some additional space next to her shop and starting a small coffee roasting business. She took samples to her coffee shop colleagues around town, as well as small retail outlets, and soon had a thriving gourmet coffee roasting business.

Then one of Jane's colleagues called one day and said they had decided to move out of state and was wondering if she was interested in buying her coffee shop?

After consulting with her Advisory Board, and with an infusion of money from her advisor friend (and some of his friends), she bought the second coffee shop and worked day and night to train and infuse in the employees of the new shop, the same culture that had made her successful from the first day at her little folding table to today.

Jane continued to learn all she could about coffee, and attended every seminar and workshop she could about running a business. She learned about hiring and managing people, how to read and understand her financial statements, and especially how to constantly maintain and update her *Planning Workbook*. Everything she did was planned out ahead of time in her little workbook.

Her Advisory Group was her guiding light, but it was her entrepreneurial spirit that pushed her on. Her passion and hard work was the foundation for the willingness of her investors, and eventually her banker, to provide the money she needed to expand her business.

After opening several coffee shops around town, and expanding her coffee roasting company substantially, her Advisory Board suggested to her one day that it was time to start talking to Venture Capitalists about helping her continue with her expansion plans.

Several VCs were interested in what she had accomplished and what her vision was for the future. They invested in

Jane and her vision, and bolstered her Corporate Board of Directors with other highly successful business people.

Java On The Fly, Inc. coffee shops then opened up all across the country, and Jane could hardly keep up with the expansion. Her little *Planning Workbook* grew and grew, but it was still her guiding manual to success.

As you would expect, the day came when the Venture Capitalists came to Jane and said it was time to consider an "Initial Public Offering" (IPO).

The end of this little story is that today Jane is CEO of one of the largest coffee house chains in the world — as well as one of the richest women in America.

Is this a fantasy story? Absolutely not!

Consider this!

Anita Roddick started by making body lotion in her kitchen and selling it to friends and neighbors who brought their own containers. She initially bootstrapped her business and was later considered by many to be the greatest woman entrepreneur in the world.

John Paul DeJoria lived in his car and cold-called on Hair Salons while peddling hair products out of the trunk of his car when he first started his business. He started out bootstrapping his business and today he is on the Forbes list of the 100 richest men in America.

Michael Dell built and sold computers to his friends while living in his dorm room at college. He started with little and bootstrapped his way up. Now Dell computers are everywhere around the world.

I could list pages and pages of success stories about highly successful people who started with absolutely nothing and bootstrapped their way to total success.

I should also point out that bootstrapping does not mean you MUST start with absolutely nothing ... you can use whatever money you have available and start further up the ladder of growth.

For instance: If Jane would have had $10,000, or so, to start her business, she probably could have initially bought her first Kiosk Coffee Cart instead of working her way up to that point. But, if she wanted the same degree of success, she would still have had to do all the research and studying that was outlined in the story.

Moreover, you don't ever HAVE to take on an investor, or seek a loan if you don't want to. *Entrepreneur Magazine's* "Entrepreneur of the Year," *Limor Fried* started her business by herself in her dorm room at college and bootstrapped her business into a $10 million a year business — without any outside investors, loans, or partners.

Limor bootstrapped her business 100% ... and there are many others out there who have successfully done exactly the same.

And, of course, not all bootstrapped businesses go all the way to an IPO. It was included in this story, because highly successful bootstrapped businesses usually do go public.

Bootstrapping a business is the truest form of entrepreneurial capitalism in action ... and anyone can do it.

Could you do the same? Could you be the Jane in the above story? Absolutely — without a doubt! This type of business startup happens every day of every year all over the world, and for every conceivable type of business.

Is it hard work? It is absolutely the hardest work there is and it is very easy to become discouraged and quit. But, as I said before, this is where the girls and boys are separated from the women and men, and only those people who are capable of hard work will become successful through **bootstrapping**.

You Too Can Do It

So, if you have a dream and no money — don't despair. If your dream is strong enough, nothing can stop you. Just open up your *Planning Workbook* and begin writing down all the things you need to do to get started. Then pick the first incremental step to get the first customer. From there on it is just a matter of using one sale to build the next, and the next, and the next, and......

That is the basic tenant of **bootstrapping**!

Summary

Well, there you have it. We've seen many ways to finance your small business ... a few of them are fairly mainstream, while others will take extremely hard work and perseverance.

If you go the Bootstrapping route, you will need to have incredible passion for your idea, unbounded patience through the entire process, and a willingness to make sacrifices while working your butt off through it all.

Obviously, Bootstrapping, or even just searching for alternative financing is very tough work. But, a recent article in Inc. Magazine pointed out that, "*... for the real entrepreneur, their business is their life. No matter the time of day, or where they're at, they cannot turn off thinking about their business. Deep passion is what makes them successful.*"

For most of us, raising money to start a new business is never an easy task. But perhaps this is a good thing, because the tremendous effort required to raise start-up money separates the "real" entrepreneurs from the "posers."

A recent study of young people age 18-30 found that over 50% of this age group would like to start a business, *if ...* the government would forgive their school loans, and make it easy for them to finance a business.

This is the group of people that should probably NOT start a business; because they obviously are not willing to work hard enough to make any business they start very successful.

I would also like to mention that, the main thread throughout this book is that ... *if you want to start a business bad enough, you can find the money – depending on how hard you want to work for it.*

Certainly not everyone has what it takes to be an entrepreneur, but if you think you do ... give it a try – you might surprise yourself.

About the Author

My name is Bob Foster and I am a small-business advisor. My background spans a few decades and is unusually eclectic in that it includes working with the smallest of small businesses as well as Fortune 100 companies.

I have worked as CEO or consultant at businesses from the high-tech world of the "Silicon Forest," to the commercial fishing grounds of Alaska and Mexico.

I've worked on projects involving products from beer to computers, and in industries from pulp and paper to urban renewal.

Along the way I earned a reputation for saving businesses that were deemed unsalvageable.

I started businesses and sold businesses, and was lied to by large multi-national corporations (according to the late *Wilson Harrell*, all big corporations lie). As an entrepreneur, I felt the excitement of success as well as the sting of failure.

Even though I spent part of my career working for large corporations, it is the small business arena that excites me — where Entrepreneurs are born and flourish.

So, that is the foundation and background upon which I am now sharing with entrepreneurs everywhere — what I learned from real experiences, not just in classrooms.

My goal is to fan the flames of the entrepreneurial spirit, and to encourage and nurture the entrepreneur in us all.

Good luck, and I wish you much success! — Bob Foster

Contact:

bob@business-solutions-and-resources.com

Website:

http://www.business-solutions-and-resources.com

www.ingramcontent.com/pod-product-compliance
Lightning Source LLC
Chambersburg PA
CBHW072038190526
45165CB00018B/1116